Jill

THE QUICKSAND BOOK

TOMIE DE PAOLA

THE QUICKSAND BOOK

SCHOLASTIC INC.
New York Toronto London Auckland Sydney Tokyo

FOR "STEVEM"
& HIS GRANDMOTHER

ISBN 0-590-32954-5

Copyright © 1977 by Tomie de Paola. All rights reserved. This edition published by Scholastic Inc., 730 Broadway, New York, N.Y. 10003, by arrangement with Holiday House, Inc.

12 11 10 9 8 7 6 5 4 3 2 1   2   4 5 6 7 8/8
Printed in the U.S.A.   07

FIRST OF ALL, QUICKSAND IS NOT A SPECIAL KIND OF SAND. IT IS PLAIN SAND. BUT WHEN WATER IS FORCED UPWARD THROUGH THE SAND, THE GRAINS ARE PUSHED APART AND THE SAND SWELLS. WHEN THIS HAPPENS, THE SAND IS NO LONGER FIRM AND CANNOT SUPPORT HEAVY WEIGHT. THAT IS WHY YOU ARE SINKING.

QUICKSAND WILL FORM ALONG SHORES OR UNDER WATER NEAR A BANK.

WATER

QUICKSAND

←SPRINGS→

←SPRINGS→

ROCK

QUICKSAND WILL SOMETIMES FORM IN MIDSTREAM.

THE SUN BAKES A THIN CRUST ON THE SAND.

ROCK

QUICKSAND

WATER

SPRING

QUICKSAND CAN FORM IN A RIVERBED THAT LOOKS DRY.

THERE IS A THIN CRUST HERE, TOO.
↓

ROCK

QUICKSAND

SPRING

JUNGLE BOY! I'M UP TO MY SHOULDERS.
HELP ME OUT!

IF YOU HAD BEEN CARRYING A STICK
OR A POLE, YOU COULD HAVE GOTTEN OUT
LIKE THIS. READ THE CHART CAREFULLY.
THESE FACTS ARE VERY HELPFUL
IF YOU ARE ALONE . . .
AND IF YOU HAVE A STICK WITH YOU.

How To Make Your Own Quicksand

① MAKE A HOLE IN THE BOTTOM OF A PAIL.

② STICK A HOSE UP THROUGH THE HOLE AND MAKE IT WATERTIGHT.

③ FILL THE PAIL 3/4 FULL WITH SAND.

④ PLACE A HEAVY OBJECT ON TOP OF THE SAND. THE OBJECT WILL STAY PUT.

⑤ TURN ON THE HOSE SO THAT A LITTLE WATER TRICKLES UP THROUGH THE SAND. THE SAND WILL SWELL AND GRAINS WILL PULL APART. WHEN THERE IS ENOUGH WATER TO MAKE THE SAND "QUICK", THE OBJECT WILL SINK.

⑥ TURN OFF THE WATER. THE SAND WILL SETTLE AND WATER WILL COME TO THE TOP. THE SAND CAN NOW HOLD ANOTHER HEAVY OBJECT. THIS IS BECAUSE THE WATER IS SQUEEZED TOWARD THE TOP, AND THE GRAINS OF SAND AREN'T PULLED APART AS MUCH.